READING & REVIEW TRACKER

THIS LOG BELONGS TO:

"READING IS MY UTOPIA."
-HELEN KELLER

CUNNINGHAM PUBLISHING: GULFPORT, MS 39503, SHEILA@SHEILAKELL.COM.

ISBN: 978-1-957587-11-0

1ST EDITION, JUNE 2024
CUNNINGHAM PUBLISHING
PUBLISHED IN THE UNITED STATES

MY FAVORITE BOOK THIS YEAR:

MY LEAST FAVORITE BOOK THIS YEAR:

READING LOG

TITLE	AUTHOR	START	END	RATING
				★★★★★
				★★★★★
				★★★★★
				★★★★★
				★★★★★
				★★★★★
				★★★★★
				★★★★★
				★★★★★
				★★★★★
				★★★★★
				★★★★★
				★★★★★
				★★★★★
				★★★★★
				★★★★★
				★★★★★
				★★★★★
				★★★★★

READING LOG

TITLE	AUTHOR	START	END	RATING
				★★★★★
				★★★★★
				★★★★★
				★★★★★
				★★★★★
				★★★★★
				★★★★★
				★★★★★
				★★★★★
				★★★★★
				★★★★★
				★★★★★
				★★★★★
				★★★★★
				★★★★★
				★★★★★
				★★★★★
				★★★★★
				★★★★★
				★★★★★

READING LOG

TITLE	AUTHOR	START	END	RATING
				★★★★★
				★★★★★
				★★★★★
				★★★★★
				★★★★★
				★★★★★
				★★★★★
				★★★★★
				★★★★★
				★★★★★
				★★★★★
				★★★★★
				★★★★★
				★★★★★
				★★★★★
				★★★★★
				★★★★★
				★★★★★
				★★★★★
				★★★★★

READING LOG

TITLE	AUTHOR	START	END	RATING
				★★★★★
				★★★★★
				★★★★★
				★★★★★
				★★★★★
				★★★★★
				★★★★★
				★★★★★
				★★★★★
				★★★★★
				★★★★★
				★★★★★
				★★★★★
				★★★★★
				★★★★★
				★★★★★
				★★★★★
				★★★★★
				★★★★★
				★★★★★

READING LOG

TITLE	AUTHOR	START	END	RATING
				★★★★★
				★★★★★
				★★★★★
				★★★★★
				★★★★★
				★★★★★
				★★★★★
				★★★★★
				★★★★★
				★★★★★
				★★★★★
				★★★★★
				★★★★★
				★★★★★
				★★★★★
				★★★★★
				★★★★★
				★★★★★
				★★★★★
				★★★★★

REVIEW TRACKER

TITLE/SERIES:

AUTHOR:

GENRE/TROPE:

START: END: DNF

HEAT
LEVEL: SWEET

RATING: ★ ★ ★ ★ ★

REVIEW

REVIEW
POSTED   GOODREADS   BOOKBUB   AMAZON   B&N   OTHER

PAPERBACK   EBOOK   AUDIO   ARC

READ AGAIN?:   YES / NO

NOTES:

REVIEW TRACKER

TITLE/SERIES:

AUTHOR:

GENRE/TROPE:

START: END: DNF

HEAT
LEVEL: SWEET

RATING:

REVIEW

REVIEW
POSTED   GOODREADS   BOOKBUB   AMAZON   B&N   OTHER

PAPERBACK   EBOOK   AUDIO   ARC

READ AGAIN?:   YES / NO

NOTES:

REVIEW TRACKER

TITLE/SERIES:

AUTHOR:

GENRE/TROPE:

START: END: DNF

HEAT LEVEL: SWEET 🌶 🌶 🌶 🌶 🌶

RATING: ⭐ ⭐ ⭐ ⭐ ⭐

REVIEW

REVIEW POSTED   GOODREADS   BOOKBUB   AMAZON   B&N   OTHER

PAPERBACK   EBOOK   AUDIO   ARC

READ AGAIN?:   YES / NO

NOTES:

REVIEW TRACKER

TITLE/SERIES:

AUTHOR:

GENRE/TROPE:

START: END: DNF

HEAT
LEVEL: SWEET

RATING: ★★★★★

REVIEW

REVIEW
POSTED   GOODREADS   BOOKBUB   AMAZON   B&N   OTHER

PAPERBACK   EBOOK   AUDIO   ARC

READ AGAIN?:   YES / NO

NOTES:

REVIEW TRACKER

TITLE/SERIES:

AUTHOR:

GENRE/TROPE:

START: END: DNF

HEAT
LEVEL: SWEET 🌶 🌶 🌶 🌶 🌶

RATING: ⭐ ⭐ ⭐ ⭐ ⭐

REVIEW

REVIEW
POSTED   GOODREADS   BOOKBUB   AMAZON   B&N   OTHER

PAPERBACK   EBOOK   AUDIO   ARC

READ AGAIN?:   YES / NO

NOTES:

REVIEW TRACKER

TITLE/SERIES:

AUTHOR:

GENRE/TROPE:

START: END: DNF

HEAT
LEVEL: SWEET 🌶 🌶 🌶 🌶 🌶

RATING: ★★★★★

REVIEW

REVIEW
POSTED   GOODREADS   BOOKBUB   AMAZON   B&N   OTHER

PAPERBACK   EBOOK   AUDIO   ARC

READ AGAIN?:   YES / NO

NOTES:

REVIEW TRACKER

TITLE/SERIES:

AUTHOR:

GENRE/TROPE:

START: END: DNF

HEAT
LEVEL: SWEET

RATING: ★★★★★

REVIEW

REVIEW
POSTED   GOODREADS   BOOKBUB   AMAZON   B&N   OTHER

PAPERBACK   EBOOK   AUDIO   ARC

READ AGAIN?:   YES / NO

NOTES:

REVIEW TRACKER

TITLE/SERIES:

AUTHOR:

GENRE/TROPE:

START: END: DNF

HEAT
LEVEL: SWEET

RATING: ★★★★★

REVIEW

REVIEW
POSTED   GOODREADS   BOOKBUB   AMAZON   B&N   OTHER

PAPERBACK   EBOOK   AUDIO   ARC

READ AGAIN?:   YES / NO

NOTES:

REVIEW TRACKER

TITLE/SERIES:

AUTHOR:

GENRE/TROPE:

START: END: DNF

HEAT
LEVEL: SWEET

RATING: ★ ★ ★ ★ ★

REVIEW

REVIEW
POSTED GOODREADS BOOKBUB AMAZON B&N OTHER

PAPERBACK EBOOK AUDIO ARC

READ AGAIN?: YES / NO

NOTES:

REVIEW TRACKER

TITLE/SERIES:

AUTHOR:

GENRE/TROPE:

START: END: DNF

HEAT
LEVEL: SWEET

RATING:

REVIEW

REVIEW   GOODREADS   BOOKBUB   AMAZON   B&N   OTHER
POSTED

PAPERBACK   EBOOK   AUDIO   ARC

READ AGAIN?:   YES / NO

NOTES:

REVIEW TRACKER

TITLE/SERIES:

AUTHOR:

GENRE/TROPE:

START: END: DNF

HEAT LEVEL: SWEET

RATING: ★★★★★

REVIEW

REVIEW POSTED   GOODREADS   BOOKBUB   AMAZON   B&N   OTHER

PAPERBACK   EBOOK   AUDIO   ARC

READ AGAIN?:   YES / NO

NOTES:

REVIEW TRACKER

TITLE/SERIES:

AUTHOR:

GENRE/TROPE:

START: END: DNF

HEAT LEVEL: SWEET

RATING: ★ ★ ★ ★ ★

REVIEW

REVIEW POSTED   GOODREADS   BOOKBUB   AMAZON   B&N   OTHER

PAPERBACK   EBOOK   AUDIO   ARC

READ AGAIN?:   YES / NO

NOTES:

REVIEW TRACKER

TITLE/SERIES:

AUTHOR:

GENRE/TROPE:

START: END: DNF

HEAT
LEVEL: SWEET 🌶 🌶 🌶 🌶 🌶

RATING: ★ ★ ★ ★ ★

REVIEW

REVIEW
POSTED   GOODREADS   BOOKBUB   AMAZON   B&N   OTHER

PAPERBACK   EBOOK   AUDIO   ARC

READ AGAIN?:   YES / NO

NOTES:

REVIEW TRACKER

TITLE/SERIES:

AUTHOR:

GENRE/TROPE:

START: END: DNF

HEAT LEVEL: SWEET 🌶 🌶 🌶 🌶 🌶

RATING: ⭐⭐⭐⭐⭐

REVIEW

REVIEW POSTED   GOODREADS   BOOKBUB   AMAZON   B&N   OTHER

PAPERBACK   EBOOK   AUDIO   ARC

READ AGAIN?:   YES / NO

NOTES:

REVIEW TRACKER

TITLE/SERIES:

AUTHOR:

GENRE/TROPE:

START:　　　　　　　　END:　　　　　　　　DNF

HEAT
LEVEL:　SWEET 🌶 🌶 🌶 🌶 🌶

RATING: ★ ★ ★ ★ ★

REVIEW

REVIEW
POSTED　　GOODREADS　　BOOKBUB　　AMAZON　　B&N　　OTHER

PAPERBACK　　EBOOK　　AUDIO　　ARC

READ AGAIN?:　YES / NO

NOTES:

REVIEW TRACKER

TITLE/SERIES:

AUTHOR:

GENRE/TROPE:

START: END: DNF

HEAT
LEVEL: SWEET

RATING: ★★★★★

REVIEW

REVIEW
POSTED   GOODREADS   BOOKBUB   AMAZON   B&N   OTHER

PAPERBACK   EBOOK   AUDIO   ARC

READ AGAIN?:   YES / NO

NOTES:

REVIEW TRACKER

TITLE/SERIES:

AUTHOR:

GENRE/TROPE:

START: END: DNF

HEAT
LEVEL: SWEET

RATING: ★★★★★

REVIEW

REVIEW
POSTED   GOODREADS   BOOKBUB   AMAZON   B&N   OTHER

PAPERBACK   EBOOK   AUDIO   ARC

READ AGAIN?:   YES / NO

NOTES:

REVIEW TRACKER

TITLE/SERIES:

AUTHOR:

GENRE/TROPE:

START: END: DNF

HEAT
LEVEL: SWEET

RATING: ★★★★★

REVIEW

REVIEW
POSTED   GOODREADS   BOOKBUB   AMAZON   B&N   OTHER

PAPERBACK   EBOOK   AUDIO   ARC

READ AGAIN?:   YES / NO

NOTES:

REVIEW TRACKER

TITLE/SERIES:

AUTHOR:

GENRE/TROPE:

START: END: DNF

HEAT
LEVEL: SWEET

RATING:

REVIEW

REVIEW
POSTED   GOODREADS   BOOKBUB   AMAZON   B&N   OTHER

PAPERBACK   EBOOK   AUDIO   ARC

READ AGAIN?:   YES / NO

NOTES:

REVIEW TRACKER

TITLE/SERIES:

AUTHOR:

GENRE/TROPE:

START: END: DNF

HEAT LEVEL: SWEET 🌶 🌶 🌶 🌶 🌶

RATING: ⭐⭐⭐⭐⭐

REVIEW

REVIEW POSTED   GOODREADS   BOOKBUB   AMAZON   B&N   OTHER

PAPERBACK   EBOOK   AUDIO   ARC

READ AGAIN?:   YES / NO

NOTES:

REVIEW TRACKER

TITLE/SERIES:

AUTHOR:

GENRE/TROPE:

START: END: DNF

HEAT
LEVEL: SWEET

RATING: ★ ★ ★ ★ ★

REVIEW

REVIEW
POSTED   GOODREADS   BOOKBUB   AMAZON   B&N   OTHER

PAPERBACK   EBOOK   AUDIO   ARC

READ AGAIN?:   YES / NO

NOTES:

REVIEW TRACKER

TITLE/SERIES:

AUTHOR:

GENRE/TROPE:

START: END: DNF

HEAT
LEVEL: SWEET

RATING:

REVIEW

REVIEW
POSTED   GOODREADS   BOOKBUB   AMAZON   B&N   OTHER

PAPERBACK   EBOOK   AUDIO   ARC

READ AGAIN?:   YES / NO

NOTES:

REVIEW TRACKER

TITLE/SERIES:

AUTHOR:

GENRE/TROPE:

START: END: DNF

HEAT
LEVEL: SWEET

RATING: ★★★★★

REVIEW

REVIEW
POSTED GOODREADS   BOOKBUB   AMAZON   B&N   OTHER

PAPERBACK   EBOOK   AUDIO   ARC

READ AGAIN?:   YES / NO

NOTES:

REVIEW TRACKER

TITLE/SERIES:

AUTHOR:

GENRE/TROPE:

START: END: DNF

HEAT LEVEL: SWEET 🌶 🌶 🌶 🌶 🌶

RATING: ★★★★★

REVIEW

REVIEW POSTED   GOODREADS   BOOKBUB   AMAZON   B&N   OTHER

PAPERBACK   EBOOK   AUDIO   ARC

READ AGAIN?:   YES / NO

NOTES:

REVIEW TRACKER

TITLE/SERIES:

AUTHOR:

GENRE/TROPE:

START: END: DNF

HEAT
LEVEL: SWEET

RATING: ★★★★★

REVIEW

REVIEW
POSTED   GOODREADS   BOOKBUB   AMAZON   B&N   OTHER

PAPERBACK   EBOOK   AUDIO   ARC

READ AGAIN?:   YES / NO

NOTES:

REVIEW TRACKER

TITLE/SERIES:

AUTHOR:

GENRE/TROPE:

START: END: DNF

HEAT
LEVEL: SWEET

RATING: ★ ★ ★ ★ ★

REVIEW

REVIEW
POSTED   GOODREADS   BOOKBUB   AMAZON   B&N   OTHER

PAPERBACK   EBOOK   AUDIO   ARC

READ AGAIN?:   YES / NO

NOTES:

REVIEW TRACKER

TITLE/SERIES:

AUTHOR:

GENRE/TROPE:

START: END: DNF

HEAT
LEVEL: SWEET

RATING: ★★★★★

REVIEW

REVIEW
POSTED   GOODREADS   BOOKBUB   AMAZON   B&N   OTHER

PAPERBACK   EBOOK   AUDIO   ARC

READ AGAIN?:   YES / NO

NOTES:

REVIEW TRACKER

TITLE/SERIES:

AUTHOR:

GENRE/TROPE:

START: END: DNF

HEAT
LEVEL: SWEET

RATING: ★★★★★

REVIEW

REVIEW
POSTED   GOODREADS   BOOKBUB   AMAZON   B&N   OTHER

PAPERBACK   EBOOK   AUDIO   ARC

READ AGAIN?:   YES / NO

NOTES:

REVIEW TRACKER

TITLE/SERIES:

AUTHOR:

GENRE/TROPE:

START: END: DNF

HEAT
LEVEL: SWEET

RATING: ★ ★ ★ ★ ★

REVIEW

REVIEW
POSTED   GOODREADS   BOOKBUB   AMAZON   B&N   OTHER

PAPERBACK   EBOOK   AUDIO   ARC

READ AGAIN?:   YES / NO

NOTES:

REVIEW TRACKER

TITLE/SERIES:

AUTHOR:

GENRE/TROPE:

START: END: DNF

HEAT
LEVEL: SWEET 🌶 🌶 🌶 🌶 🌶

RATING: ★ ★ ★ ★ ★

REVIEW

REVIEW
POSTED   GOODREADS   BOOKBUB   AMAZON   B&N   OTHER

PAPERBACK   EBOOK   AUDIO   ARC

READ AGAIN?:   YES / NO

NOTES:

REVIEW TRACKER

TITLE/SERIES:

AUTHOR:

GENRE/TROPE:

START: END: DNF

HEAT
LEVEL: SWEET

RATING: ★ ★ ★ ★ ★

REVIEW

REVIEW
POSTED   GOODREADS   BOOKBUB   AMAZON   B&N   OTHER

PAPERBACK   EBOOK   AUDIO   ARC

READ AGAIN?:   YES / NO

NOTES:

REVIEW TRACKER

TITLE/SERIES:

AUTHOR:

GENRE/TROPE:

START: END: DNF

HEAT
LEVEL: SWEET

RATING:

REVIEW

REVIEW
POSTED   GOODREADS   BOOKBUB   AMAZON   B&N   OTHER

PAPERBACK   EBOOK   AUDIO   ARC

READ AGAIN?:   YES / NO

NOTES:

REVIEW TRACKER

TITLE/SERIES:

AUTHOR:

GENRE/TROPE:

START: END: DNF

HEAT LEVEL: SWEET

RATING: ★ ★ ★ ★ ★

REVIEW

REVIEW POSTED   GOODREADS   BOOKBUB   AMAZON   B&N   OTHER

PAPERBACK   EBOOK   AUDIO   ARC

READ AGAIN?:   YES / NO

NOTES:

REVIEW TRACKER

TITLE/SERIES:

AUTHOR:

GENRE/TROPE:

START: END: DNF

HEAT LEVEL: SWEET

RATING:

REVIEW

REVIEW POSTED   GOODREADS   BOOKBUB   AMAZON   B&N   OTHER

PAPERBACK   EBOOK   AUDIO   ARC

READ AGAIN?:   YES / NO

NOTES:

REVIEW TRACKER

TITLE/SERIES:

AUTHOR:

GENRE/TROPE:

START: END: DNF

HEAT
LEVEL: SWEET

RATING: ★★★★★

REVIEW

REVIEW
POSTED   GOODREADS   BOOKBUB   AMAZON   B&N   OTHER

PAPERBACK   EBOOK   AUDIO   ARC

READ AGAIN?:   YES / NO

NOTES:

REVIEW TRACKER

TITLE/SERIES:

AUTHOR:

GENRE/TROPE:

START: END: DNF

HEAT LEVEL: SWEET 🌶 🌶 🌶 🌶 🌶

RATING: ⭐ ⭐ ⭐ ⭐ ⭐

REVIEW

REVIEW POSTED   GOODREADS   BOOKBUB   AMAZON   B&N   OTHER

PAPERBACK   EBOOK   AUDIO   ARC

READ AGAIN?:   YES / NO

NOTES:

REVIEW TRACKER

TITLE/SERIES:

AUTHOR:

GENRE/TROPE:

START: END: DNF

HEAT
LEVEL: SWEET

RATING: ★★★★★

REVIEW

REVIEW
POSTED   GOODREADS   BOOKBUB   AMAZON   B&N   OTHER

PAPERBACK   EBOOK   AUDIO   ARC

READ AGAIN?:   YES / NO

NOTES:

REVIEW TRACKER

TITLE/SERIES:

AUTHOR:

GENRE/TROPE:

START: END: DNF

HEAT
LEVEL: SWEET

RATING:

REVIEW

REVIEW
POSTED   GOODREADS   BOOKBUB   AMAZON   B&N   OTHER

PAPERBACK   EBOOK   AUDIO   ARC

READ AGAIN?:   YES / NO

NOTES:

REVIEW TRACKER

TITLE/SERIES:

AUTHOR:

GENRE/TROPE:

START: END: DNF

HEAT
LEVEL: SWEET

RATING: ★★★★★

REVIEW

REVIEW
POSTED   GOODREADS   BOOKBUB   AMAZON   B&N   OTHER

PAPERBACK   EBOOK   AUDIO   ARC

READ AGAIN?:   YES / NO

NOTES:

REVIEW TRACKER

TITLE/SERIES:

AUTHOR:

GENRE/TROPE:

START: END: DNF

HEAT
LEVEL: SWEET

RATING: ★★★★★

REVIEW

REVIEW   GOODREADS   BOOKBUB   AMAZON   B&N   OTHER
POSTED

PAPERBACK   EBOOK   AUDIO   ARC

READ AGAIN?:   YES / NO

NOTES:

REVIEW TRACKER

TITLE/SERIES:

AUTHOR:

GENRE/TROPE:

START: END: DNF

HEAT
LEVEL: SWEET

RATING:

REVIEW

REVIEW
POSTED   GOODREADS   BOOKBUB   AMAZON   B&N   OTHER

PAPERBACK   EBOOK   AUDIO   ARC

READ AGAIN?:   YES / NO

NOTES:

REVIEW TRACKER

TITLE/SERIES:

AUTHOR:

GENRE/TROPE:

START: END: DNF

HEAT
LEVEL: SWEET

RATING: ★★★★★

REVIEW

REVIEW
POSTED   GOODREADS   BOOKBUB   AMAZON   B&N   OTHER

PAPERBACK   EBOOK   AUDIO   ARC

READ AGAIN?:   YES / NO

NOTES:

REVIEW TRACKER

TITLE/SERIES:

AUTHOR:

GENRE/TROPE:

START: END: DNF

HEAT
LEVEL: SWEET

RATING: ★ ★ ★ ★ ★

REVIEW

REVIEW
POSTED   GOODREADS   BOOKBUB   AMAZON   B&N   OTHER

PAPERBACK   EBOOK   AUDIO   ARC

READ AGAIN?:   YES / NO

NOTES:

REVIEW TRACKER

TITLE/SERIES:

AUTHOR:

GENRE/TROPE:

START: END: DNF

HEAT LEVEL: SWEET

RATING: ★★★★★

REVIEW

REVIEW POSTED   GOODREADS   BOOKBUB   AMAZON   B&N   OTHER

PAPERBACK   EBOOK   AUDIO   ARC

READ AGAIN?:   YES / NO

NOTES:

REVIEW TRACKER

TITLE/SERIES:

AUTHOR:

GENRE/TROPE:

START: END: DNF

HEAT LEVEL: SWEET

RATING: ⭐⭐⭐⭐⭐

REVIEW

REVIEW POSTED   GOODREADS   BOOKBUB   AMAZON   B&N   OTHER

PAPERBACK   EBOOK   AUDIO   ARC

READ AGAIN?:   YES / NO

NOTES:

REVIEW TRACKER

TITLE/SERIES:

AUTHOR:

GENRE/TROPE:

START: END: DNF

HEAT
LEVEL: SWEET 🌶️ 🌶️ 🌶️ 🌶️ 🌶️

RATING: ⭐⭐⭐⭐⭐

REVIEW

REVIEW
POSTED   GOODREADS   BOOKBUB   AMAZON   B&N   OTHER

PAPERBACK   EBOOK   AUDIO   ARC

READ AGAIN?:   YES / NO

NOTES:

REVIEW TRACKER

TITLE/SERIES:

AUTHOR:

GENRE/TROPE:

START: END: DNF

HEAT LEVEL: SWEET

RATING: ★★★★★

REVIEW

REVIEW POSTED   GOODREADS   BOOKBUB   AMAZON   B&N   OTHER

PAPERBACK   EBOOK   AUDIO   ARC

READ AGAIN?:   YES / NO

NOTES:

REVIEW TRACKER

TITLE/SERIES:

AUTHOR:

GENRE/TROPE:

START: END: DNF

HEAT
LEVEL: SWEET

RATING:

REVIEW

REVIEW
POSTED   GOODREADS   BOOKBUB   AMAZON   B&N   OTHER

PAPERBACK   EBOOK   AUDIO   ARC

READ AGAIN?:   YES / NO

NOTES:

REVIEW TRACKER

TITLE/SERIES:

AUTHOR:

GENRE/TROPE:

START: END: DNF

HEAT
LEVEL: SWEET 🌶 🌶 🌶 🌶 🌶

RATING: ⭐⭐⭐⭐⭐

REVIEW

REVIEW
POSTED   GOODREADS   BOOKBUB   AMAZON   B&N   OTHER

PAPERBACK   EBOOK   AUDIO   ARC

READ AGAIN?:   YES / NO

NOTES:

REVIEW TRACKER

TITLE/SERIES:

AUTHOR:

GENRE/TROPE:

START: END: DNF

HEAT
LEVEL: SWEET

RATING: ★ ★ ★ ★ ★

REVIEW

REVIEW
POSTED   GOODREADS   BOOKBUB   AMAZON   B&N   OTHER

PAPERBACK   EBOOK   AUDIO   ARC

READ AGAIN?:   YES / NO

NOTES:

REVIEW TRACKER

TITLE/SERIES:

AUTHOR:

GENRE/TROPE:

START: END: DNF

HEAT LEVEL: SWEET 🌶 🌶 🌶 🌶 🌶

RATING: ★★★★★

REVIEW

REVIEW POSTED GOODREADS BOOKBUB AMAZON B&N OTHER

PAPERBACK EBOOK AUDIO ARC

READ AGAIN?: YES / NO

NOTES:

REVIEW TRACKER

TITLE/SERIES:

AUTHOR:

GENRE/TROPE:

START: END: DNF

HEAT
LEVEL: SWEET

RATING: ★ ★ ★ ★ ★

REVIEW

REVIEW
POSTED   GOODREADS   BOOKBUB   AMAZON   B&N   OTHER

PAPERBACK   EBOOK   AUDIO   ARC

READ AGAIN?:   YES / NO

NOTES:

REVIEW TRACKER

TITLE/SERIES:

AUTHOR:

GENRE/TROPE:

START: END: DNF

HEAT
LEVEL: SWEET

RATING:

REVIEW

REVIEW
POSTED   GOODREADS   BOOKBUB   AMAZON   B&N   OTHER

PAPERBACK   EBOOK   AUDIO   ARC

READ AGAIN?:   YES / NO

NOTES:

REVIEW TRACKER

TITLE/SERIES:

AUTHOR:

GENRE/TROPE:

START: END: DNF

HEAT
LEVEL: SWEET

RATING:

REVIEW

REVIEW
POSTED   GOODREADS   BOOKBUB   AMAZON   B&N   OTHER

PAPERBACK   EBOOK   AUDIO   ARC

READ AGAIN?:   YES / NO

NOTES:

REVIEW TRACKER

TITLE/SERIES:

AUTHOR:

GENRE/TROPE:

START: END: DNF

HEAT
LEVEL: SWEET

RATING: ⭐⭐⭐⭐⭐

REVIEW

REVIEW
POSTED   GOODREADS   BOOKBUB   AMAZON   B&N   OTHER

PAPERBACK   EBOOK   AUDIO   ARC

READ AGAIN?:   YES / NO

NOTES:

REVIEW TRACKER

TITLE/SERIES:

AUTHOR:

GENRE/TROPE:

START: END: DNF

HEAT
LEVEL: SWEET 🌶 🌶 🌶 🌶 🌶

RATING: ⭐ ⭐ ⭐ ⭐ ⭐

REVIEW

REVIEW
POSTED   GOODREADS   BOOKBUB   AMAZON   B&N   OTHER

PAPERBACK   EBOOK   AUDIO   ARC

READ AGAIN?:   YES / NO

NOTES:

REVIEW TRACKER

TITLE/SERIES:

AUTHOR:

GENRE/TROPE:

START: END: DNF

HEAT
LEVEL: SWEET

RATING: ⭐⭐⭐⭐⭐

REVIEW

REVIEW
POSTED   GOODREADS   BOOKBUB   AMAZON   B&N   OTHER

PAPERBACK   EBOOK   AUDIO   ARC

READ AGAIN?:   YES / NO

NOTES:

REVIEW TRACKER

TITLE/SERIES:

AUTHOR:

GENRE/TROPE:

START: END: DNF

HEAT
LEVEL: SWEET

RATING: ★ ★ ★ ★ ★

REVIEW

REVIEW
POSTED   GOODREADS   BOOKBUB   AMAZON   B&N   OTHER

PAPERBACK   EBOOK   AUDIO   ARC

READ AGAIN?:   YES / NO

NOTES:

REVIEW TRACKER

TITLE/SERIES:

AUTHOR:

GENRE/TROPE:

START:　　　　　　END:　　　　　　DNF

HEAT
LEVEL:　SWEET 🌶 🌶 🌶 🌶 🌶

RATING: ★ ★ ★ ★ ★

REVIEW

REVIEW
POSTED　　GOODREADS　　BOOKBUB　　AMAZON　　B&N　　OTHER

PAPERBACK　　EBOOK　　AUDIO　　ARC

READ AGAIN?:　YES / NO

NOTES:

REVIEW TRACKER

TITLE/SERIES:

AUTHOR:

GENRE/TROPE:

START: END: DNF

HEAT LEVEL: SWEET

RATING: ★ ★ ★ ★ ★

REVIEW

REVIEW POSTED   GOODREADS   BOOKBUB   AMAZON   B&N   OTHER

PAPERBACK   EBOOK   AUDIO   ARC

READ AGAIN?:   YES / NO

NOTES:

REVIEW TRACKER

TITLE/SERIES:

AUTHOR:

GENRE/TROPE:

START: END: DNF

HEAT
LEVEL: SWEET

RATING:

REVIEW

REVIEW
POSTED   GOODREADS   BOOKBUB   AMAZON   B&N   OTHER

PAPERBACK   EBOOK   AUDIO   ARC

READ AGAIN?:   YES / NO

NOTES:

REVIEW TRACKER

TITLE/SERIES:

AUTHOR:

GENRE/TROPE:

START: END: DNF

HEAT
LEVEL: SWEET

RATING: ★ ★ ★ ★ ★

REVIEW

REVIEW
POSTED   GOODREADS   BOOKBUB   AMAZON   B&N   OTHER

PAPERBACK   EBOOK   AUDIO   ARC

READ AGAIN?:   YES / NO

NOTES:

REVIEW TRACKER

TITLE/SERIES:

AUTHOR:

GENRE/TROPE:

START: END: DNF

HEAT
LEVEL: SWEET 🌶 🌶 🌶 🌶 🌶

RATING: ★ ★ ★ ★ ★

REVIEW

REVIEW
POSTED   GOODREADS   BOOKBUB   AMAZON   B&N   OTHER

PAPERBACK   EBOOK   AUDIO   ARC

READ AGAIN?:   YES / NO

NOTES:

REVIEW TRACKER

TITLE/SERIES:

AUTHOR:

GENRE/TROPE:

START: END: DNF

HEAT
LEVEL: SWEET

RATING:

REVIEW

REVIEW
POSTED   GOODREADS   BOOKBUB   AMAZON   B&N   OTHER

PAPERBACK   EBOOK   AUDIO   ARC

READ AGAIN?:   YES / NO

NOTES:

REVIEW TRACKER

TITLE/SERIES:

AUTHOR:

GENRE/TROPE:

START: END: DNF

HEAT
LEVEL: SWEET

RATING: ★★★★★

REVIEW

REVIEW
POSTED   GOODREADS   BOOKBUB   AMAZON   B&N   OTHER

PAPERBACK   EBOOK   AUDIO   ARC

READ AGAIN?:   YES / NO

NOTES:

REVIEW TRACKER

TITLE/SERIES:

AUTHOR:

GENRE/TROPE:

START: END: DNF

HEAT
LEVEL: SWEET

RATING: ⭐⭐⭐⭐⭐

REVIEW

REVIEW
POSTED   GOODREADS   BOOKBUB   AMAZON   B&N   OTHER

PAPERBACK   EBOOK   AUDIO   ARC

READ AGAIN?:   YES / NO

NOTES:

REVIEW TRACKER

TITLE/SERIES:

AUTHOR:

GENRE/TROPE:

START: END: DNF

HEAT
LEVEL: SWEET

RATING: ★★★★★

REVIEW

REVIEW
POSTED   GOODREADS   BOOKBUB   AMAZON   B&N   OTHER

PAPERBACK   EBOOK   AUDIO   ARC

READ AGAIN?:   YES / NO

NOTES:

REVIEW TRACKER

TITLE/SERIES:

AUTHOR:

GENRE/TROPE:

START: END: DNF

HEAT
LEVEL: SWEET

RATING:

REVIEW

REVIEW
POSTED   GOODREADS   BOOKBUB   AMAZON   B&N   OTHER

PAPERBACK   EBOOK   AUDIO   ARC

READ AGAIN?:   YES / NO

NOTES:

REVIEW TRACKER

TITLE/SERIES:

AUTHOR:

GENRE/TROPE:

START: END: DNF

HEAT
LEVEL: SWEET

RATING: ★★★★★

REVIEW

REVIEW   GOODREADS   BOOKBUB   AMAZON   B&N   OTHER
POSTED

PAPERBACK   EBOOK   AUDIO   ARC

READ AGAIN?:   YES / NO

NOTES:

REVIEW TRACKER

TITLE/SERIES:

AUTHOR:

GENRE/TROPE:

START: END: DNF

HEAT
LEVEL: SWEET

RATING:

REVIEW

REVIEW
POSTED   GOODREADS   BOOKBUB   AMAZON   B&N   OTHER

PAPERBACK   EBOOK   AUDIO   ARC

READ AGAIN?:   YES / NO

NOTES:

REVIEW TRACKER

TITLE/SERIES:

AUTHOR:

GENRE/TROPE:

START: END: DNF

HEAT LEVEL: SWEET

RATING: ★★★★★

REVIEW

REVIEW POSTED   GOODREADS   BOOKBUB   AMAZON   B&N   OTHER

PAPERBACK   EBOOK   AUDIO   ARC

READ AGAIN?:   YES / NO

NOTES:

REVIEW TRACKER

TITLE/SERIES:

AUTHOR:

GENRE/TROPE:

START: END: DNF

HEAT LEVEL: SWEET 🌶 🌶 🌶 🌶 🌶

RATING: ⭐ ⭐ ⭐ ⭐ ⭐

REVIEW

REVIEW POSTED   GOODREADS   BOOKBUB   AMAZON   B&N   OTHER

PAPERBACK   EBOOK   AUDIO   ARC

READ AGAIN?:   YES / NO

NOTES:

REVIEW TRACKER

TITLE/SERIES:

AUTHOR:

GENRE/TROPE:

START: END: DNF

HEAT
LEVEL: SWEET

RATING: ★★★★★

REVIEW

REVIEW
POSTED   GOODREADS   BOOKBUB   AMAZON   B&N   OTHER

PAPERBACK   EBOOK   AUDIO   ARC

READ AGAIN?:   YES / NO

NOTES:

REVIEW TRACKER

TITLE/SERIES:

AUTHOR:

GENRE/TROPE:

START: END: DNF

HEAT LEVEL: SWEET

RATING: ⭐⭐⭐⭐⭐

REVIEW

REVIEW POSTED   GOODREADS   BOOKBUB   AMAZON   B&N   OTHER

PAPERBACK   EBOOK   AUDIO   ARC

READ AGAIN?:   YES / NO

NOTES:

REVIEW TRACKER

TITLE/SERIES:

AUTHOR:

GENRE/TROPE:

START: END: DNF

HEAT
LEVEL: SWEET

RATING: ★ ★ ★ ★ ★

REVIEW

REVIEW
POSTED   GOODREADS   BOOKBUB   AMAZON   B&N   OTHER

PAPERBACK   EBOOK   AUDIO   ARC

READ AGAIN?:   YES / NO

NOTES:

REVIEW TRACKER

TITLE/SERIES:

AUTHOR:

GENRE/TROPE:

START: END: DNF

HEAT
LEVEL: SWEET

RATING:

REVIEW

REVIEW
POSTED   GOODREADS   BOOKBUB   AMAZON   B&N   OTHER

PAPERBACK   EBOOK   AUDIO   ARC

READ AGAIN?:   YES / NO

NOTES:

REVIEW TRACKER

TITLE/SERIES:

AUTHOR:

GENRE/TROPE:

START: END: DNF

HEAT
LEVEL: SWEET

RATING: ★ ★ ★ ★ ★

REVIEW

REVIEW
POSTED   GOODREADS   BOOKBUB   AMAZON   B&N   OTHER

PAPERBACK   EBOOK   AUDIO   ARC

READ AGAIN?:   YES / NO

NOTES:

REVIEW TRACKER

TITLE/SERIES:

AUTHOR:

GENRE/TROPE:

START: END: DNF

HEAT
LEVEL: SWEET

RATING: ★ ★ ★ ★ ★

REVIEW

REVIEW
POSTED   GOODREADS   BOOKBUB   AMAZON   B&N   OTHER

PAPERBACK   EBOOK   AUDIO   ARC

READ AGAIN?:   YES / NO

NOTES:

REVIEW TRACKER

TITLE/SERIES:

AUTHOR:

GENRE/TROPE:

START: END: DNF

HEAT
LEVEL: SWEET

RATING: ★★★★★

REVIEW

REVIEW
POSTED   GOODREADS   BOOKBUB   AMAZON   B&N   OTHER

PAPERBACK   EBOOK   AUDIO   ARC

READ AGAIN?:   YES / NO

NOTES:

REVIEW TRACKER

TITLE/SERIES:

AUTHOR:

GENRE/TROPE:

START: END: DNF

HEAT
LEVEL: SWEET 🌶 🌶 🌶 🌶 🌶

RATING: ⭐ ⭐ ⭐ ⭐ ⭐

REVIEW

REVIEW
POSTED   GOODREADS   BOOKBUB   AMAZON   B&N   OTHER

PAPERBACK   EBOOK   AUDIO   ARC

READ AGAIN?:   YES / NO

NOTES:

REVIEW TRACKER

TITLE/SERIES:

AUTHOR:

GENRE/TROPE:

START: END: DNF

HEAT
LEVEL: SWEET

RATING: ★★★★★

REVIEW

REVIEW
POSTED   GOODREADS   BOOKBUB   AMAZON   B&N   OTHER

PAPERBACK   EBOOK   AUDIO   ARC

READ AGAIN?:   YES / NO

NOTES:

REVIEW TRACKER

TITLE/SERIES:

AUTHOR:

GENRE/TROPE:

START: END: DNF

HEAT
LEVEL: SWEET 🌶 🌶 🌶 🌶 🌶

RATING: ⭐ ⭐ ⭐ ⭐ ⭐

REVIEW

REVIEW
POSTED   GOODREADS   BOOKBUB   AMAZON   B&N   OTHER

PAPERBACK   EBOOK   AUDIO   ARC

READ AGAIN?:   YES / NO

NOTES:

REVIEW TRACKER

TITLE/SERIES:

AUTHOR:

GENRE/TROPE:

START: END: DNF

HEAT
LEVEL: SWEET

RATING: ★ ★ ★ ★ ★

REVIEW

REVIEW
POSTED   GOODREADS   BOOKBUB   AMAZON   B&N   OTHER

PAPERBACK   EBOOK   AUDIO   ARC

READ AGAIN?:   YES / NO

NOTES:

REVIEW TRACKER

TITLE/SERIES:

AUTHOR:

GENRE/TROPE:

START: END: DNF

HEAT
LEVEL: SWEET

RATING: ★ ★ ★ ★ ★

REVIEW

REVIEW
POSTED   GOODREADS   BOOKBUB   AMAZON   B&N   OTHER

PAPERBACK   EBOOK   AUDIO   ARC

READ AGAIN?:   YES / NO

NOTES:

REVIEW TRACKER

TITLE/SERIES:

AUTHOR:

GENRE/TROPE:

START: END: DNF

HEAT
LEVEL: SWEET

RATING: ★★★★★

REVIEW

REVIEW
POSTED   GOODREADS   BOOKBUB   AMAZON   B&N   OTHER

PAPERBACK   EBOOK   AUDIO   ARC

READ AGAIN?:   YES / NO

NOTES:

REVIEW TRACKER

TITLE/SERIES:

AUTHOR:

GENRE/TROPE:

START: END: DNF

HEAT LEVEL: SWEET 🌶 🌶 🌶 🌶 🌶

RATING: ⭐ ⭐ ⭐ ⭐ ⭐

REVIEW

REVIEW POSTED   GOODREADS   BOOKBUB   AMAZON   B&N   OTHER

PAPERBACK   EBOOK   AUDIO   ARC

READ AGAIN?:   YES / NO

NOTES:

REVIEW TRACKER

TITLE/SERIES:

AUTHOR:

GENRE/TROPE:

START: END: DNF

HEAT LEVEL: SWEET

RATING: ★ ★ ★ ★ ★

REVIEW

REVIEW POSTED   GOODREADS   BOOKBUB   AMAZON   B&N   OTHER

PAPERBACK   EBOOK   AUDIO   ARC

READ AGAIN?:   YES / NO

NOTES:

REVIEW TRACKER

TITLE/SERIES:

AUTHOR:

GENRE/TROPE:

START: END: DNF

HEAT
LEVEL: SWEET

RATING:

REVIEW

REVIEW
POSTED   GOODREADS   BOOKBUB   AMAZON   B&N   OTHER

PAPERBACK   EBOOK   AUDIO   ARC

READ AGAIN?:   YES / NO

NOTES:

REVIEW TRACKER

TITLE/SERIES:

AUTHOR:

GENRE/TROPE:

START: END: DNF

HEAT
LEVEL: SWEET

RATING: ★ ★ ★ ★ ★

REVIEW

REVIEW   GOODREADS   BOOKBUB   AMAZON   B&N   OTHER
POSTED

PAPERBACK   EBOOK   AUDIO   ARC

READ AGAIN?:   YES / NO

NOTES:

REVIEW TRACKER

TITLE/SERIES:

AUTHOR:

GENRE/TROPE:

START: END: DNF

HEAT LEVEL: SWEET

RATING:

REVIEW

REVIEW POSTED   GOODREADS   BOOKBUB   AMAZON   B&N   OTHER

PAPERBACK   EBOOK   AUDIO   ARC

READ AGAIN?:   YES / NO

NOTES:

REVIEW TRACKER

TITLE/SERIES:

AUTHOR:

GENRE/TROPE:

START: END: DNF

HEAT
LEVEL: SWEET

RATING: ★★★★★

REVIEW

REVIEW
POSTED   GOODREADS   BOOKBUB   AMAZON   B&N   OTHER

PAPERBACK   EBOOK   AUDIO   ARC

READ AGAIN?:   YES / NO

NOTES:

REVIEW TRACKER

TITLE/SERIES:

AUTHOR:

GENRE/TROPE:

START: END: DNF

HEAT LEVEL: SWEET 🌶🌶🌶🌶🌶

RATING: ⭐⭐⭐⭐⭐

REVIEW

REVIEW POSTED   GOODREADS   BOOKBUB   AMAZON   B&N   OTHER

PAPERBACK   EBOOK   AUDIO   ARC

READ AGAIN?: YES / NO

NOTES:

REVIEW TRACKER

TITLE/SERIES:

AUTHOR:

GENRE/TROPE:

START: END: DNF

HEAT
LEVEL: SWEET 🌶 🌶 🌶 🌶 🌶

RATING: ⭐⭐⭐⭐⭐

REVIEW

REVIEW
POSTED   GOODREADS   BOOKBUB   AMAZON   B&N   OTHER

PAPERBACK   EBOOK   AUDIO   ARC

READ AGAIN?:   YES / NO

NOTES:

REVIEW TRACKER

TITLE/SERIES:

AUTHOR:

GENRE/TROPE:

START: END: DNF

HEAT
LEVEL: SWEET

RATING:

REVIEW

REVIEW
POSTED   GOODREADS   BOOKBUB   AMAZON   B&N   OTHER

PAPERBACK   EBOOK   AUDIO   ARC

READ AGAIN?:   YES / NO

NOTES:

REVIEW TRACKER

TITLE/SERIES:

AUTHOR:

GENRE/TROPE:

START: END: DNF

HEAT
LEVEL: SWEET

RATING: ★★★★★

REVIEW

REVIEW
POSTED   GOODREADS   BOOKBUB   AMAZON   B&N   OTHER

PAPERBACK   EBOOK   AUDIO   ARC

READ AGAIN?:   YES / NO

NOTES:

REVIEW TRACKER

TITLE/SERIES:

AUTHOR:

GENRE/TROPE:

START: END: DNF

HEAT
LEVEL: SWEET

RATING: ★ ★ ★ ★ ★

REVIEW

REVIEW
POSTED   GOODREADS   BOOKBUB   AMAZON   B&N   OTHER

PAPERBACK   EBOOK   AUDIO   ARC

READ AGAIN?:   YES / NO

NOTES:

REVIEW TRACKER

TITLE/SERIES:

AUTHOR:

GENRE/TROPE:

START: END: DNF

HEAT
LEVEL: SWEET

RATING: ★ ★ ★ ★ ★

REVIEW

REVIEW
POSTED   GOODREADS   BOOKBUB   AMAZON   B&N   OTHER

PAPERBACK   EBOOK   AUDIO   ARC

READ AGAIN?:   YES / NO

NOTES:

REVIEW TRACKER

TITLE/SERIES:

AUTHOR:

GENRE/TROPE:

START: END: DNF

HEAT
LEVEL: SWEET 🌶 🌶 🌶 🌶 🌶

RATING: ★ ★ ★ ★ ★

REVIEW

REVIEW
POSTED   GOODREADS   BOOKBUB   AMAZON   B&N   OTHER

PAPERBACK   EBOOK   AUDIO   ARC

READ AGAIN?:   YES / NO

NOTES:

REVIEW TRACKER

TITLE/SERIES:

AUTHOR:

GENRE/TROPE:

START: END: DNF

HEAT
LEVEL: SWEET

RATING: ★ ★ ★ ★ ★

REVIEW

REVIEW
POSTED   GOODREADS   BOOKBUB   AMAZON   B&N   OTHER

PAPERBACK   EBOOK   AUDIO   ARC

READ AGAIN?:   YES / NO

NOTES:

REVIEW TRACKER

TITLE/SERIES:

AUTHOR:

GENRE/TROPE:

START: END: DNF

HEAT
LEVEL: SWEET

RATING:

REVIEW

REVIEW
POSTED   GOODREADS   BOOKBUB   AMAZON   B&N   OTHER

PAPERBACK   EBOOK   AUDIO   ARC

READ AGAIN?:   YES / NO

NOTES:

Made in the USA
Columbia, SC
09 October 2024